C000133626

Edited by: Penny Thresher, Corner House Words

Cover design by: Miriam Husby Stener

Creative Illustrations by: Lauren Cyprien

Author photography by: Aamod Korhonen & Sophelia Korhonen

ISBN: 9798770798913

Imprint: Independently published

This book is dedicated to my three children Ofelia, Cornelius & Julius. Becoming your mother made me realize the power of unconditional love and sent me out on a journey of spiritual awakening.

I also dedicate this book to my greatest spiritual teachers Anni Sennov and Dr. Erin Fall Haskell.

You where the leaders, when I was searching for answers.

Thank you Anni for encouraging me to be my own guru, believing in me and sharing all your wisdom about new time energy and the four elements. For guiding me in how to find my Dharma and making it fun!

Thank you Dr.Erin for building the best community of spiritual entrepreneurs, for being my teacher in New Thought and spiritual psychology coaching, for helping me release the limited beliefs that stood in the way for living my purpose and mission, and for learning me to live my truth!

This book is created because you showed me the way to play my own game of divinity.

Forever grateful!

Miriam

CONTENTS

FOREWORD

The poems in this book are written during
the year I studied to become a New Thought
Spiritual Practitioner, 2020-2021.

In my class, there where students with different back-
grounds.
Some from church, others from no church at all.

For me, these teachings meant a total shift in seeing the
world and how everything is created. Coming from a
background of Humanism, I had a really big resistance
to the word GOD.

During this year my perspective changed.

Shifting from believing GOD was some man in the sky
to
feeling GOD within me, knowing GOD was all creation
and I was one with GOD was a total crack in my previous
belief system. All of a sudden the concept of GOD was
less triggering.
It all made sense!

One way I see the world is through poetry. When I need to understand something, I put my thoughts on a piece of paper and it becomes more clear.

If you are at the start of your spiritual awakening, maybe some of the words I use might feel strange to you. Perhaps you noticed I used the word GOD 6 times on the previous page.
I encourage you to have a taste of the words, see if they will grow on you during the reading. Luckily we all get to create our own experiences.

If you are already embodying these teachings, swimming in the divine ocean, as Rumi so eloquently say:

You are not a drop in the ocean; you are the entire ocean in a drop

I hope these poems will encourage you to keep on swimming.

I would like to finish this foreword with one of my favorite New Thought quotes, by Thomas Troward:

The purpose of life is to enjoy life.

Whatever reason brought you to hold this book in your hands, or read these lines online, I truly hope you will enjoy it!

With love,
Miriam

WHO AM I?

1.

On the bridge
Between the worlds

She stood
And looked out on the world

Feeling
She did not belong

Lost on the bridge
Between the worlds

She did not yet know
It was her gift
To know them both

2.

She did not have a bad day
She was just disconnected
from the source within
Manifesting as the effect of life
And not the
spiritual badass
That she truly was

3.

What if we are here,
To create heaven on earth?
What if our soul chose for us to come here
and that spirit got choked,
realising what it had chosen?
What if it felt deceived and manipulated?

What if this frustration
was the spark
That took it on a journey
in a search for meaning,
a search for purpose
a reason WHY it chose to land in a body
On this strange planet called earth?

What if this search
Led to
What the soul already knew

It is the designer
Of its own life

4.

I never understood Job's book.
Why all the suffering?
Why all the losses?

I asked God
-Why did he have to lose it all,
to get your gift?

God replied
-He did not.
He just realised he had nothing to lose.
You do not have to give up anything.
You just have to remember.
You are all of it.

5.

I looked at the world and got confused
I was feeling peace within
What I saw was war

If who I Am
Is what I create
How can I be looking at war?

How can I have created this?
How can I un-create it?
This is not what I want to look at!

I said this,
to the One Mind,
when we drank coffee in my garden,
together with Mrs. Peace.

- I am sorry but I have to leave you,
said Mrs. Peace

I do not want you to leave, I told her.

Why do you want Mrs. Peace to stay? the One Mind
asked me

I like her company, I told him.

Why are you directing your energy on the war?

Because there is war in the world.

Is there?

I was finding The One Mind a bit annoying at this
time and answered him in an upset tone;
Of course there is war. Look at all the damage it is
causing!

Do you believe you are divine? The One Mind asked me
in a neutral tone.

Yes of course I am.

Do you believe everything is divine?

Yes I do believe that.

Even war?

No, of course not. Wars are horrific. They are evil.

How do you believe wars got created?

It started in the mind of human beings. And then was
manifested into form.

Yes, the creative process in action! Do you believe all
human beings are divine?

At this point, I started feeling that the One Mind
was tricking me into a game I was about to lose.
Yes I do.

My dear friend, when you change your perception
of what is divine and what is not, the world you
see will change. When you see that everything is
created from the same source, well actually - by me,
no honour taken, you see the divine in everything.

All of you have the power to create both heaven on
earth as well as hell. You are one with everything
ever created. Even wars. You have the freedom to
use your energy to create whatever you want.
I am at your service. Tell me what you believe, and I will
create it for you.

Want to use your powers to fight something you do not
like, then Mrs. Peace might not want to stick around.

Want to use it to build something you want to enjoy, I
promise you, Mrs. Peace will be there cheering you on.

So you mean I can create peace, and still look at war?

Exactly! Because war will be the meaning you give it. If
it is your divine calling to create peace, you will do that
and there will be less wars. If it is not your calling, then
trying to fight wars will only give you war inside. And
more wars externally. You are the creator. You get to

decide what life you want to create.

Ok, I think I got it. And Mrs. Peace, thank you for not leaving the party.

Ooo my pleasure. Thanks for inviting me to stay. Now, let's eat some of those delicious cakes!

You mean those with a lot of sugar in them...?

The One Mind looked at me, and rolled his neutral eyes.

Was even sugar divine? I decided not to fight sugar. My energy was needed for another calling.

Yes and No. You get to choose. Some are raw and full of nutrition, others, well they are pure sweet and sugar, honey! You can even have both!

Perfect! Lets eat cakes and enjoy this party!!

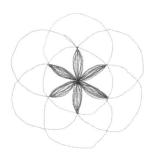

6.

The music started playing
And I opened my eyes
From a sleep
In the darkness

The music played
In Sad sad tones
No glimpse of joy
Twisting my body
In uncomfortable movements

-NO!!
I screamed!
This is not the melody I want today,
I stopped listening
And went into prayer

The clouds in my mind
danced into the sky
When I spoke the words
of Truth
of Love
or Law

Rewriting the melody

Into a song
I enjoyed dancing to

I am the music and the movement
The musician and the dancer
Playing the song
of my soul
And so it is.

7.

That GAH feeling
Came for a visit
I had not invited it

What if I pretend it is not here?
Play happy and ignore
The baffling pressure
It put on my chest

Hey you GAH!

I really do not have time for visitors now.
I am in the middle of creating
The life of my dreams!
I turned around.
But it was everywhere!

Hey you GAH!

Which part of
"I am trying to ignore you"
Do you not understand?

It did not answer
It just stayed

What the fuck do you want?

Why are you even here?

To get you to the next level.

To let you feel me
I am not here to stay
Unless you keep ignoring me
I am just passing by
For you to take the next step
I will stay
Until you do your inner work
And see the truth

All feelings are divinely created
Not as punishments
But as divine guidance
For you to understand
How you can grow
Love and joy
Are just as divine
as anger and frustration
We are all made from
The same fountain
of life
Inside of you.
We are not against you
We are not here to bother you
We are here to express
What you believe
In the present moment
As quickly as we come
We can go

Listening to the sound
Of the GAH feeling

Something started changing
The words became quieter
The pressure dissipated
And was replaced with
Another visitor
Miss Gratefulness.

8.

When the footprints
of who I am
got washed away by the ocean
as I walked with you

I realised
I am not my steps
I am not my marks.
Who am I?
To you?

Some call you God
Some call you Source.
Who are you?
To me?

I see you
far away from me
I feel you
far away
from me

They say
I am a drop
carrying the ocean
within me
Like I am
the ocean
washing it away

Some call you God
Some call you Source
Who am I?
To you?

When the footprints
of who I am
got washed away
by the ocean
I felt truth
in me

I see you
you are here with me
I feel you
you are her in me
Mir*
I am

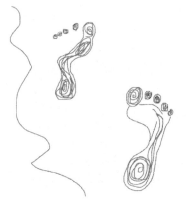

*Mir = Peace, and also my name Miriam divided into the I am identity;

Mir I am

I AM NATURE

9.

Nature speaks
The language of all times

Look at the beauty of a lilac
its seducing sweet smell
It's power to heal

The word lack
Is not
a word
In the mind of a lilac

Even if it blooms
Only a short, short time
It always blooms again
The next year

Like it has no awareness of time
Only of its purpose

10.

I see your light
The clear and bright light that is yours
A twinkling star in the darkest winter night

You are not alone,
do you know that?

One by one we get lit
Together we create a bright shining night
with every star shining its own light

You are a twinkling star
We are the starry sky

11.

Disconnect to connect
Disconnect from the wifi
Go out in nature
Connect
to the infinite Abundance
To the richness
To the growth
To the peace and harmony
The stillness and the storm
The dead leaves that give life to the
soil of the next season
Beauty and destruction
All of it
Together
In the circle of infinite life

Close your eyes,
And feel,

You are one with all life.
You are nature!

12.

We never lost
spirituality
on earth
we just did not see
Through the fog in our mind

When the sky is clear
We will awaken
To a new time of creation

13.

An old oak
stood in the garden
Observing life passing by

-   I wonder if nature
has many lives?
The young soul asked his mother,
walking by the old oak.

When his mother couldn't give him an answer,
the old oak whispered softly with the wind
Only the child could hear
Its old voice of wisdom;
-We are all nature,
One with time
Eternal
And forever living

We will always be here
Just like you,
my child

14.

What is a miracle?

How strange to see the darkness disappear
within the glimpse
of a few seconds
when a bright flash
made the night bright

I asked my friend
Did you see the light in the sky?

She had not seen it,
but she told me an oak had spoken to her the other day
Shared its words of wisdom on the question;
What is the purpose of creation?

The old oak told her
It is not the final product that matter
The result is not the reason we create
When we focus on the end result,
we do not see that
creation is not a finished product
Creation is all of it

The process of creation
The joy of creating
The inspired action
Planting the seeds
Nurturing
Harvesting

Loving the process
Enjoying all of it

That is the purpose
Of creation

This is the power
that helps darkness
to disappear
In the flash
Of a few seconds!

15.

My friend talking to an oak
Inspired me
to talk to the old oak
Standing
in front of my house

I hugged it
And asked
What information do you have for me?

The earth.
was its reply

I felt disappointed
Not understanding the message

The next day I went back
Said hello and gave it a hug
I asked again,
but this time
I asked the question
In another way

Is there anything I need to know for my highest good?

You people struggle so much,

You do not have to
it replied

How do we not struggle?

With the firmness and wisdom of an old oak,
seeing people come and go,
it calmly replied

You just stop doing it.

All of a sudden the message
from the day before
made sense

The earth!

Nature does not struggle
It follows the rhythm
and transformes
with the seasons
It does not resist
It do not struggle
To hold on to summer,
when it is time for fall

I thanked the oak
for sharing its wisdom
Of non resistance

16.

Tonight
The stars shine
Brightly in the dark
Dancing with the moon
Of light

The night
Was created
For you to rest
So you can be awake

Energy never sleeps
Your dreams are made of infinity
Planted in the dark soil of the night
And born
Into the bright light of day

17.

After a long cold winter
The songbirds are singing
a symphony
where every note is different

My bare skin
Smells like sun
I enjoy
The warm and gentle heat

I wish I could be
like summer
All year long

The Scandinavian nature
Laughs and sends me a smile
An tells me
It does not intend to change
Its nature
For my benefit

It wants to change
With the seasons
Bloom in the summer
And rest in the winter

We are both so
Changeable and

Adjustable

After a long cold winters rest
We can bloom
And sing together again
With the songbirds
Arriving from Southern Europe

If we don't like the tones
Of a season
The expression
Of nature
We are always free
To create another song
And move
Where our song
Can sing freely
In harmony
With our true nature

18.

The Peony
decided to bloom

Giving us the gift
of its beauty

Soon it's time
as a flower
will be over

While it visits
it asks us gently

- Enjoy the gift
of my beauty

19.

Come to the fountain
And drink
the water
of life

Let the water
remind you
of who you are
and what you carry

You are the feelings
The emotions
creating
into form

You are the water
You drink
Every thought you water
will bloom into life
In your sacred garden of Eden

20.

The rhythm of a moon so full
brought the water
to flood

A wave of tsunami
hit my body
cleansing it
washing away all the dirt
preventing me from seeing clearly

I am the holy water
poured into a cup of tea
Drinking it with Jesus
As i am God
In all and ever present.

I AM PLEASURE, PASSION & JOY

21.

When pleasure
Got labeled
as Sin

She lost
A piece of herself

When the divine truth
cleansed her blood
And revealed
There was never
a thing called sin
Only
The misuse
Of energy

She could feel
How the heat
made her blush
And then

She took it
She enjoyed it

The door
To her soul
was open
And she stepped in

22.

Where there is a fire
let it burn
Be the light in the night
For those asleep

Let it burn
And unite with the flames
Of passion, truth and desire

23.

The fire of life
danced through her
She embraced
The power
To burn it all down
or
Rise like a Pheonix
With truth burning in her heart
Lifting her up on her wings

She was the flame
And could burn
Wherever She wanted

24.

I paint
My life with
Words

And dance
To the rhythm of my soul

I AM TRUTH

25.

What is this word TRUTH?
She asked the voice within

Truth,
is knowing the nature of who you are
The lyrics in the song of the Uni Verse
The harmony of divine principles
That which knows the absolute

God is everything
In everything
The core
of who you are

Truth is all you believe
Truth is all you do not believe
The unveiling
of all that has ever been
and ever will be
Truth is knowing who you are
And knowing, you are all of it

26.

Truth is truth
When it is
And when it isn't

The truth was triggering
So I closed my eyes

It was not my preferred truth
So I told it to fuck of
When it continued to bother me

I got so mad at it
And walked away

Don't you think the bastard followed?
Whispering words of truth in my ears.

If I accepted its company
I had to deal with reality
Of truth being truth

I wasn't ready for that,
Yet.

I AM FEMININE & MASCULINE

27.

The wounded feminine
asked
the wounded masculine
to protect her
and got hurt

The divine feminine
knows
she is always protected
by the law
of her beliefs

The masculine
is not
the cause
of safety
She is

28.

With the seed
Of divine masculine
Creation starts

Implanting
Into
The womb
Of the divine feminine
For her
To give birth
To baby creation
In form

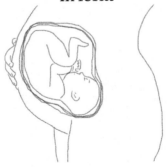

There is no separation
Between the two of them
Together they create
Together they birth
And unite
In the sacred process
Of creating life into form

I AM LOVE

29.

I love
Because
I am love

30.

They tried to put love in a box
They did not know
Love cannot be contained!

Love is eternal
Love is vibration
Traveling through time and space
Knowing no borders

Love cannot be contained!

It loves
Because it is Love

If you have a desire inside of you
To love someone
To love yourself

Let this feeling be free
And be proud
Of your ability to Love

Because really,
You cannot put love in a box!

31.

If all I ever did
was love
then that would be enough

If all I ever felt
was gratitude
then that would be enough

If the only truth I knew
was that I am divine
one with all
then I would know
I will always be enough

I AM MOVEMENT

32.

I travel through
time and space
with the speed
of consciousness

I visit a memory
from ancient times
and it feels
so real
as if it was
This very present moment

Stored in my cells
as a memory
to be revealed
and healed
with the speed
of consciousness
and the truth of time

33.

As tiny particles
In space
We are drifting
Towards unknown destinations
By a force
Stronger
Than our material

34.

I am
Completion
The first and the last

a wanderer
On a path of no endings

Together with you

I travel this journey
As spirit
manifested into form

I am brave
And walk where my soul desires

When needed
I make new paths

And I dance fiercely
With the waves of the northern lights

I am fully and freely alive
In every moment

I make the most
of every present moment
Right NOW

When my dance is over
I say goodbye to my body

Knowing
I was here

And I enjoyed it!

I loved every part of the journey
As a spirit in form

I AM DIVINE

35.

Those battles inside
Fighting their way
Into divinity

Through darkness and pain
Feeling less worth
Like a fraud
A disappointment
And no one cares

Battling darkness
Inside of you
Knowing to lose,
Is to surrender

Having Faith
That falling down
Will not hurt
As much
As never letting go
Of the need
To fight for your right
To be accepted

But in that fall,
You will see
That believing
That you are divine

Is all you ever need

No matter what goes on
Internally
Externally

Seeing with your clear eyes
That this fight
Is nothing
But a distraction
Keeping you
From seeing
the truth of who you are

And that is all of it

Playing
Both sides of the battle
As one

And you can never lose
The game of your divinity

36.

Only inner riches
can be taken with you
when you die

37.

The Form
Will change
It can even disappear

The soul
Has eternal life

Why do so many
Want to hold on
To the form
The material
That is doomed
at one time
To no longer exist?

38.

I want to be cradled
Like a newborn
In my cave of the divine feminine

Feeling safe
Feeling protected
Feeling loved

By the energy of all times

Shifting
my energy
from needing to knowing
Shifting the thought
Into truth
I see

I already am
Safe
protected
Loved
In spirit
In body

By my own belief
And connection
To the soul
Of who

I am

I AM GRATEFUL

39.

With gratefulness
I sow the seeds
To grow in my garden of
Eden

I water them
with love
with faith
with truth
with passion
and with joy

Seeing them grow

makes me realize
This garden is me
Blooming in divinity

40.

In this moment
I empty my mind
and fill my heart
with gratitude

I am so grateful for this day
The creative process
And the law of cause and effect
Always creating
Moments to be grateful for
Family, friends, nature and animals
My life, body and soul
To love and enjoy life

I am so grateful that I am created
And that i get to create
Thank you, thank you, thank you.

I AM FREEDOM

41.

The very first breath of freedom
Was waiting for me
To breathe

I held my breath for so long
waiting for someone
to release it

I could not
hold it any more
Decided
To breathe
to the rhythm of freedom
Inhaling the air of truth
Exhaling the clouds keeping me from knowing

I am always free to breathe!

I AM ONENESS

42.

My I AM
Is ONE
With
your I AM

Judging you
Is judging me

Loving You
Is loving Me

When one of us rises
We ALL rise

Together
as ONE

43.

I Release
The bond of suffering
Of right
Or wrong

I am not divided

The Black night
Is the other side
Of the Light day

Polarities
Are created
By the ONE Source
Trying on
Different expressions

44.

I searched outside
In the land of effects
For love, joy and happiness

I did not know
I was the cause
Of the life I lived

I did not know
Christ within
Was the way
That lead to God
The source
Of all creation

When I realized
Christ, God and me
Where old friends
We belonged together
As One team
I knew
I never had to search again

45.

I am harmony
singing
The ONE song
from within

All the tones
in this Uni Verse
I sing

I am the music
I am the tones
I am the words
in harmony
with this ONE song
we all are singing

I AM SILENCE

46.

In silence
I hear
Without words

I AM POETRY

47.

I am
A piece of poetry
Changing form
As time goes by

Written words
from the depths of my soul
Creating me
Into form

Some lines shine brightly in the sky
and some wander in the dark
And some fill up quietly in between

Empty paper
Waiting to be filled
With pages
Never written before

I am
a piece of poetry
A masterpiece of art
Created in the book of life

Individual Unique Loved

masterpiece divine
I am Poetry I am art
love
free
free

creative source

I AM

48.

The lost child
Found home
Where
The
Source
Was

49.

I found myself
floating
in the air of possibility

The law is infinite
It flows right through
In the noise of silence

I am

50.

I am energy
created into form
by the words
once spoken

Gracefully I bring
my pain & suffering to mould
into the divine Diamond
I am

Shining brightly
as a body
a piece of heaven
dancing barefoot in the grass

Thank you body
for giving my spirit a home

51.

I am
The creative process
Creating
Everything
Into form

This poem
Is the form
These words
Are the form

Created By law
Filtered through
The subjective mind
Of Mir I am
And into the existence
For you to read

52.

I am the truth
I am the way
I am the life

The words from the Bible
Echo
In my mind

A spark
Had lit my heart
And I heard them for the very first time

I am
Not outside of me

The way, the truth and the life
Was always
To be found
In the very essence
Of these words

I AM

53.

I AM
The Christ Consciousness
The light to the darkness
Loving both as one

You are no sinner
There was never
A thing called sin
Only forgetting
You are whole and complete

You are
The perfect image
Of me

Bring your light
And shine Your Glory
You are perfect
The way you create!

54.

I recognize
This source
Creating all art
The artist of heaven
The earth
The stars
The Dance
And the northern lights
The painters
And their paintings
All expressions of creation
This source created you
It created me
To write these words
For you to read
I am the artist
I am the art
Both poetry and poet
I am a glimpse
of the masterpiece
Of creation
Creating my masterpiece
And so are you!

55.

I got many names
Been to many places
Singing many songs
Dancing to the rhythms of many lives

I am to you
What you believe me to be

If you call
I will answer

I am everywhere
Past, present and future
This very moment

I am the stars you see at night
I am the fields of gold
And the diamonds in your eyes

I am all emotions
The first glimpse of sun in the morning
And the forces of nature destroying cities like Pompeii

I am destruction
I am life

I am the words in this book
The poems
And the Chapters

I am nature
I am pleasure, passion, joy
I am truth

I am feminine & masculine
I am love
I am movement
I am divine
I am grateful
I am freedom
I am Oneness
I am silence
I AM

RESOURCES

This book is created to help you on your way to knowing the truth of who you are. As a thank you for getting your copy, I have created the Ultimate Truth guide for you.
Go here to download it:

https://miriamstener.mykajabi.com/ultimate-truth-guide

It is so much more fun to live your truth together. Come join The Divine Dance Club on Facebook:

https://www.facebook.com/groups/171458348411545

SOCIAL MEDIA

INSTAGRAM:
@miriamstener & @miriamhstener

FACEBOOK:
https://www.facebook.com/miriamhstener

YOUTUBE:
https://www.youtube.com/channel/
UC3si2CU1tbX61X92xqr29gw

WEBSITE:
https://miriamstener.mykajabi.com/

CONTACT INFORMATION:
Email: hej@miriamstener.se

ABOUT THE AUTHOR

Miriam Husby Stener

 Miriam is a spiritual psychology coach and a New Thought spiritual practitioner. Born in Norway, but is currently living in Sweden.

She is the founder of the podcast and Youtube channel The Divine Dance Club, which is about concious conversations with women who listen to the music within and decided to dance to their souls expression.

Miram is passionate about helping female soulpreneurs dance from their soul, heal their traumas so that they can live their truth, passions, creative expressions, purpose and calling.

Miriam is educated to university standard with her education in political science, language, communication, finances, conflict management and is currently studying to become a New Thought teacher and Dr. Divinity in New Thought Global and Soulciété.

She started her career in the online stock market at a Bank in Stockholm.

Becoming a mother in 2009 she felt there was a missing part in her life and she began her spiritual journey.

Miriam's mission is to help women world wide learn how to create their own heaven on earth, overcoming traumas and see the divine truth of who they truly are.

Printed in Great Britain
by Amazon

74384587R00068